HOW TO WRITE A LETTER

FLORENCE D. MISCHEL

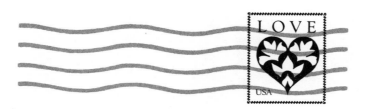

HOW TO WRITE A LETTER

Illustrated by Anne Canevari Green

A First Book Revised Edition
Franklin Watts / 1988

New York/ London/ Toronto/ Sydney

Excerpt from *Memoirs, Volume I: Year of Decisions* by
Harry S. Truman. Published by Doubleday, New York. Copyright
© 1955. Reprinted by permission of Margaret Truman Daniel.

First published as *The First Book of Letter Writing*
by Helen Jacobson and Florence D. Mischel, 1957.

Library of Congress Cataloging-in-Publication Data

Mischel, Florence.
How to write a letter / by Florence Mischel ; illustrated by Anne
Canvari Green — Rev. ed., 2nd ed.
p.   cm.—(A First Book)
Rev. ed. of: The first book of letter writing / Helen Jacobson and
Florence Mischel. 1957.
Includes index.
Summary: Discusses the importance of letter writing as a means of
prompt and in-depth communication, from sharing experiences with
family and friends to expressing opinions to government officials
and others. Includes advice on writing business and friendly letters
and information on postage, punctuation, and addresses.
ISBN 0-531-10587-3
1. Letter-writing—Juvenile literature.   [1. Letter writing.]
I. Green, Anne Canevari, Ill.   II. Jacobson, Helen. First book of
letter writing.   III. Title.   IV. Series.
BJ2101.M5   1988
395'.4—dc19   88-10263   CIP   AC

For my grandchildren:
Rafe, Becca, and Jesse

CONTENTS

HOW TO WRITE A LETTER

——— WHY WE WRITE LETTERS ———

Not so many years ago, if you wrote to your friends or relatives many miles away, weeks or even months might go by before you could get an answer. Today your letters can travel even to faraway places in a few days.

Before we had the telephone, letter writing was the main way friends and families kept in touch with one another. Despite advances in communication, the letters we write are the most lasting way to stay close to our friends and family.

Writing letters is really just "talking on paper." You can't save the conversations you have on the telephone, but if the letter you receive is special, you can read it over and over again. If a letter comes when you are busy, or do not have privacy, you can put it away until a better time. You can also write things in a letter that may be too hard to say.

Some people find it difficult to write letters. But we learn many things by doing them again and again, and that includes letter writing. Once you have the habit of writing letters you will have learned a skill you will need and enjoy all your life.

Letters provide a way to share experiences with your friends, and letters also give them an opportunity to share their interests with you.

An even better reason for writing letters is that letter writing can be fun. It will be more fun if you don't let too much time pass before you answer your friends' letters. Learn to write right away. The more often you see your friends, the more things you have to talk about, and the more you enjoy doing things together. It's the same with writing letters. The more often you exchange letters with your friends, the more things you will find to share.

The secret of a good letter writer is being able to speak naturally on paper. Even though we say that writing letters is just talking on paper, there are some things we don't do when we write that we may do when we talk. We don't ramble and hesitate on paper, or repeat the same phrase over and over again as we sometimes do in talking. We can't use our hands or faces to show how we feel. We have to find words that will do it.

It takes more time to put words on paper than it does to say them aloud. This gives us a chance to plan what we are going to say. We can "think out" an idea before we write the words, and that often means that we are able to say it better.

In this way we begin to develop a "style" of writing. Style in writing is the expression of your own personality. The letter you write shows something of you—the way you sound and think. That is why when you write to a friend your letter is a gift of your friendship.

Since writing letters is really just talking on paper, let's look at how some young people talk to each other.

———— TALKING ON PAPER ————

Have you ever received a letter that said absolutely nothing? For example:

Dear Jim,

How are you? I am fine. Write soon.

> So long,
> *Bill*

If you wrote back

Dear Bill,

I am glad you are fine. I am fine too.
Please write me again.

> Your friend,
> *Jim*

your correspondence could end there.

When you speak with your friends in person or on the telephone, you tell them about things you have been doing and you listen to the news your friends have to tell. The letter you write is your half of a conversation by mail. A good letter has something to say. It is an expression of who you are, and of your personality. So, be yourself in writing it.

How much more fun it is to receive a letter like this. And how much easier to answer.

498 Olinton Avenue
Bronx, New York 10461
August 21, 1988

Dear Raoul,

Well, we are finally unpacked!!! I thought we would be living out of boxes forever. But here we are—two whole weeks before school begins! Our new apartment is really rad, man. There are four buildings in the project, with about a hundred apartments all together. Each building has grass and trees around it and some have benches in a tiny park. In the middle, there's a slide and sandbox for little kids like my sister Bessie.

Remember how sore I was when we moved? But honestly, Raoul, it is great. I don't know many kids yet but I see some my age around and I guess I'll meet more when school starts.

I got your card from camp. Was that goofball Eddie there this year? There's a big "Y" near my new school and I hear they've got a good basketball team. I'm going to try out.

I really miss you, Raoul. My mom is going to buy bunk beds from a lady in our building and she says I can have friends visit during vacations. Will you come?

'Bye for now. Tell everyone hello for me.

Your friend,
Shabkah

Box 468
Kennebunkport, Maine 04014
August 4, 1988

Dear Nora,

In two weeks I am coming home, so write me back at my mother's house. You be sure now!

I am having a good time here but I don't think I would like to live in the country all the time. It is very quiet and at night it is very, very dark. The mosquitos are terrible. At first I couldn't stand them, but my stepmother gave me some vitamins or else I got used to them or maybe they went away.

I have been to the beach three times. My father and his wife took me. Her name is Veronica but he calls her Rony. She is going to have a baby. She is nice but I still feel funny sometimes.

What did you do this summer? Are you having fun? Did your cousin Piggy-Peggy come? Do you like her now? I read four Nancy Drew books. Veronica said she read them when she was my age—can you imagine! I didn't think they had Nancy Drew books back then, but she says that all they did was change some of the expressions.

Nora, if I don't find a letter from you when I get home, I am going to be really mad. You won't believe this, but I can't wait for school to start.

Much love,
Judy

These letters contain enough news to give Raoul and Nora things to talk about. And there are enough questions to show the writers' interest in hearing about *their* experiences. A good letter, then, follows a few simple rules.

1. Tell about yourself.

2. Be interested in what your friend is doing.

3. Share your experiences. Make your friends want to answer so that they can hear from you again.

4. Be yourself. Let your letter be an expression of your personality.

5. Write right away. It is always easier to reply to a letter if you do not let it get stale.

Some people like to save their letters. Whether you save your letters or not, it is a good idea to keep them until you have answered them. In that way, you can read your friends' letters again and make sure you have answered all their questions and said something about what your friends have written.

HOW WE WRITE LETTERS

Just as styles have changed in the way we dress and travel and talk, so has the style changed in the way we write.

Not so long ago it was the fashion to be quite elaborate. For example, this is how one man closed a letter two hundred years ago:

> With very great esteem and regard,
> I have the honor to be, dear Sir,
> Your obedient Servant
> *Alexander Hamilton*

Today we express ourselves more naturally and without fussiness, both in speech and on paper. But there are still some forms we follow so that the persons receiving the letters can read and understand them more easily.

There are two types of letters. A letter written to a friend or relative is called a *friendly* letter. A letter written to someone you don't know is usually a *business* letter. Some letters are a combination of both. The rules for writing a business letter are more formal than the rules for writing a friendly letter.

Although throughout this book we stress that you should be yourself and express your own personality, you should learn letter forms. After you know them, and understand why we use them, you can decide whether you want to ignore some rules when you write to your close friends and family. Remember, though, that letters you write to people you do not know, to casual friends and family members whom you rarely see, should follow the standard forms.

THE FORM FOR FRIENDLY LETTERS

There are five parts to a friendly letter:

1. The heading
2. The salutation
3. The body of the letter
4. The close
5. The signature

The Heading

The heading gives your address and the date on which you began your letter. It is written on the right-hand half of the paper, about an inch from the top. Start the heading in the center of the page so that you will have room to finish each line. Your street address is written on the first line. On the next line, flush (even) with the line above, write the name of your city, the name of your state, and your zip code. On the third line, write the date.

Spell out the name of the month when you write the date. Do not use numerals. In this country, we write the month first, followed by the date and year. Place a comma between the date and the year.

March 5, 1988

In many parts of the world, the date is written by putting the day of the month first, then the month and year. No commas are needed when the date is written this way.

5 March 1988

If you used numerals to write this date in the United States, it would be 3/5/88, but in Europe it would be written 5/3/88. So avoid confusion by writing out the name of the month.

The heading makes it easier for your reader to reply. Even if your friends know your address, they may not remember the zip code. Besides, the heading is a good hint to your friend that you expect a reply.

You will know best whether you need to include your address in the heading when you write to close friends and family. Just be sure to include the date so your readers will know when you wrote, especially if they happen to save letters. You may be famous some day and it will be important to know when you wrote your letters!

The Salutation

The beginning of a letter is called the salutation. This word comes from the verb "to salute," which means to greet. When you meet a friend you say "Hello," or "Hi." When you write a letter you also start with a greeting.

It is easier to read a letter if there is a border of empty space on each side of the page. These borders are called the margins. Leave a border for the left-hand margin—perhaps an inch of space—and then start the salutation. The salutation should be written a line or two below the heading.

The Body of the Letter

The salutation is the way you begin the letter. The body of the letter is what you have to say in the letter, and what it

207 East 25th Ave.
Eugene, Oregon 97403
November 2, 1988

Dear Josh,

How are you? Is college hard? My school is OK, so far.

We watched your football team on television Saturday. Mom was sad that you didn't get to play, but we saw you on the bench. Dad says you'll get to play next year.

Our hockey tryouts start Monday. Is it all right if I use your hockey stick?

When are you coming home?

Love,
Tim

is depends upon the person to whom you are writing. Not every friendship is the same, so you may write about different things to different people. Because your letter is an expression of who you are, only you can decide what to say in a letter and how to say it. The only rule to follow is: Be yourself.

The Close

The close of a letter is the part where you say good-by in writing. The close depends on how you feel about the person to whom you are writing. For example, a letter to your best friend might close like this:

> With much love,
> *Lisa*

When you are writing to someone you do not know very well, you might sign the letter with your full name:

> Sincerely,
> *Julie Timpone*

The Signature

Whether you use your first name or your full name, the signature must always be handwritten.

Postscripts

P.S. is an abbreviation for postscript and comes from the Latin phrase *post scriptum,* which means "after something written." Postscripts are not one of the five parts of a letter, but they may be added on.

If you have forgotten to write something in the body of your letter, put the letters, P.S. at the left-hand margin on the line below your signature, and add your message.

With much love,
Rebecca Ella

P.S. I forgot to tell you that Beeko is going to have puppies next week. I get to have my pick of the litter.

THE FORM FOR BUSINESS LETTERS

A business letter has six parts. All the parts should be included in every business letter. Business letters are more formal than letters to your friends. Use plain paper, write in ink or type, and follow the standard rules.

The parts of a business letter are:

1. The heading
2. The inside address
3. The salutation
4. The body of the letter
5. The close
6. The signature

The Heading

The heading includes your address and the date on which your letter is written.

The Inside Address

The inside address includes the name of the person to whom you are writing, if you know it; the name of the company or organization where the person works; and the address. Begin the first line of the inside address at the left margin about two line spaces or more below your heading. Each line is written directly below the line above. Leave a line space before the salutation.

The Salutation

You remember that the salutation is the way you open the conversation by saying "hello."

If you are writing to a company and do not know the name of the man or woman who will be reading your letter, you may use the person's title.

Dear Director:
Dear Complaint Department:
Dear Editor:

If you do know the name of the person, address a man as Mr. and a woman as Ms. Until a few years ago, a woman was addressed as Mrs. if she was married, or Miss if she was not. A man was, and is, called Mr. whether he is married or single. Many people feel that a woman should have the same privacy about her personal life. So, unless you know that a woman prefers to be addressed as Mrs. or Miss, it is good form to use Ms.

Dear Ms. Clements:
Dear Mr. Levine:

Dear Dr. Bunim:
Dear Prof. Howes:
Dear Mrs. Krivetsky:

Whichever salutation you use, it must always be followed by a colon (:) in a business letter. Leave a line space between the salutation and the body.

The Body of the Letter

First, decide what your letter is about. Explain why you are writing in the opening paragraph. Describe your business simply and keep your letter brief and to the point. It will get more attention that way. Business people are often busy.

The Close

There are several ways of closing a business letter. Whichever form you choose, follow your close with a comma. Skip a line before the close.

Yours truly,
Cordially,
Sincerely,
Yours sincerely,

The Signature

Sign your name below the close. Always write out your name in full. Do not abbreviate. Do not write Chas. Conklin. If you like, you may use only the initial of your first name, as C. Conklin. It is better, however, to write Charles Conklin.

If you type your letter, type your name four line spaces under the close. Sign your name by hand in the space between the close and your typed name.

Yours truly,

Charles Conklin

Charles Conklin

ALL ABOUT ENVELOPES

Whether you are sending a business letter or a friendly letter, the envelope is prepared in the same way.

Addressing the Envelope

Unless an envelope is addressed clearly and properly, your letter may be delayed. It may even end up in the dead-letter box of the post office and never be delivered at all.

Put the name of the person you are writing to on the first line; the building or house number and the street address on the second line; and the city, state, and zip code on the third line. Start writing the address in the center of the envelope, about halfway down from the top. Begin each line exactly under the line above.

If the address is made up of just numbers, separate the house number from the street number with a dash (–).

1172–43 Street

The Return Address

You may make a mistake in addressing an envelope. Or perhaps your friend has moved. If the post office knows where you live, it will return your letter. That is why you put your own address on the envelope too.

You may write the return address on the back flap of the envelope, or on the face (front) of the envelope. The post office prefers the return address in the upper left-hand corner of the face of the envelope and most people do it that way. It should be done that way for business letters.

Can you guess why the post office prefers a return address on the *face* of the envelope?

The Stamp

The stamp is placed at the right-hand top corner of the envelope.

The Zip Code

Most countries use some form of zip code. Zip codes help to speed delivery of the mail. If you forget to put the zip code on the envelope, it may take the post office more time to deliver your letter.

Perhaps it will help you remember to use zip codes if you know what they mean. The zip codes shown in this book have five digits. Each digit in the zip code provides a piece of information.

The United States Post Office has divided the country, including its territories, into ten large geographic areas, numbered from 0 to 9. The first digit of each zip code stands for one of these large areas. For example, zip codes for Puerto Rico and the northeastern states begin with zero. The western states and Hawaii and Alaska have zips beginning with 9. The second and third numbers in a zip identify a city or a part of a state. The last two digits identify the local post office station or post office branch that serves the area.

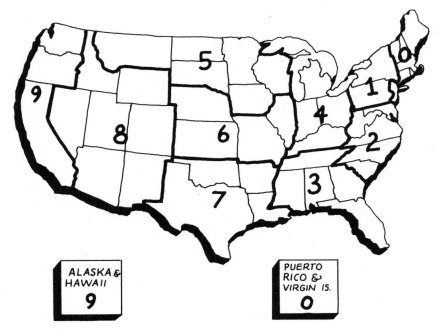

As an example, let us take the address 235 Montgomery Street in San Francisco. The zip code for this address is 94104. The number 9 tells the postal clerk who is sorting mail that the letter is going to the westernmost part of the country. The numbers 41 show that the addressee (the person who is going to get the letter) lives in San Francisco. The last two numbers, 04, show that the mail will be delivered from a local post office station called Rincon North.

The Post Office has now added an additional four digits to zip codes. These numbers narrow the delivery areas to smaller and smaller sections within a city or town. The full 9-digit zip code numbers are now used mainly by large companies, like electric or telephone companies. The Post Office has automated equipment that can read the zip codes.

It saves postal employees many long hours of sorting mail by hand. Handwritten and typed envelopes are still sorted by hand. The Post Office prefers that you place the zip code number after the name of the state so that the postal clerk can see it easily and can separate the mail more quickly.

If you do not know a zip code, there are directories at the post office and in libraries, or the post office workers can help you. In some states, telephone books include zip code information.

SPELLING, PUNCTUATION, AND OTHER TRICKY MATTERS

Spelling

Very often your mind races ahead faster than you can write. So before you mail your letter, read it over to be sure you haven't left out words.

And watch your spelling! English is a rich language but it is difficult too. It is not surprising if you do not know how to spell a word. But you can look it up in a dictionary, to make sure that your friend will understand what you write.

Punctuation

Punctuation is a system of using marks like periods (.), commas (,), and question marks (?) to make it easier to understand the written words. Each sentence ends with a

punctuation mark, usually a period. When your sentences are very long, you may need commas to separate the phrases so that the meaning is clear.

As a general rule, you use punctuation marks in writing in the places where you would pause if you were speaking.

You will find some rules about letter punctuation in the back of this book. The main thing to remember is that punctuation marks are used to make your meaning clear.

Abbreviations

An abbreviation is a shortened form of a word—for example, *Sat.* for Saturday. Abbreviations should not be used in the body of a letter except for words like Mr., Mrs., Ms., Dr., and a few other well-known abbreviations for names that are very long. Abbreviations of institutions, broadcasting networks, unions, and well-known organizations may be written in capital letters without periods.

Federal Bureau of Investigation	FBI
United States of America	USA

National Association for the Advancement of Colored People	NAACP
Union of Soviet Socialist Republics	USSR
National Football League	NFL

Except for such well-known abbreviations, you should always spell out your words. In that way, you can be sure your meaning will be clear.

If you look in the dictionary you will see that one abbreviation may have many meanings. Here is an example:

SS	special police unit of the Nazi Party
ss	shortstop (in baseball)
SS	Steamship
SS	Saints

You may, if you like, use abbreviations in the heading and inside address.

Street	St.
Avenue	Ave.
Place	Pl.
Road	Rd.

The abbreviations for every state in the Union are listed at the end of this book, but it is better not to abbreviate the names of states when you address your envelopes by hand. The abbreviations of many state names look alike and unless your handwriting is very clear, and you also include the correct zip code, the post office may have difficulty guessing the name of the state.

Numbering Pages

If your letter is more than one page, you need to number each page after the first one.

Handwriting

Schools teach cursive writing. This is handwriting in which all the letters of a single word are joined together.

Schools usually first teach students to use a form of printing. Each letter in a word is unconnected, and separated from its neighbors.

When you write letters, use the kind of writing that is most comfortable for you. The important thing is that your writing must be legible, that is, easy to read.

Typewriter or Personal Computer

You may be using a typewriter or a personal computer to write your letters. The signature, in friendly or business letters, must be handwritten.

Some people who type their letters like to add a handwritten note. The story is told that President Franklin Delano Roosevelt used to cross out a word or the close on some of his typewritten letters and add something else in his own handwriting. He did this so that people would feel that, busy as he was, he had given their letter his personal attention.

STATIONERY AND POSTAGE

Stationery

Once you begin writing letters, you may enjoy choosing stationery. Some people prefer a single, unfolded sheet of paper, plain white or colored; some prefer folded stationery with four sides. If you have printed stationery, you may want your name and address on it, just your address, or only your name or initials.

The paper should be folded to fit the envelope, usually in half or thirds. Full-size sheets, such as typing paper, are folded in thirds to fit a large (business size) envelope. For a small envelope, the sheet is folded in half and then in thirds. You will be able to tell how to fold the paper from the way it fits into the envelope. If you slide your letter into the envelope with the cut side down and the folded side up, it is easier to remove.

Postage

Many men and women work many hours to deliver your letters. So the United States Post Office sells stamps to help pay the costs of delivering the mail. Stamps are pasted on the upper right-hand corner of the envelope.

The amount of postage you need will depend on where your letter is going, how much it weighs, and the kind of delivery you want.

Letters are usually sent by first-class mail. If you want your letter to be delivered especially fast, you can send it by express mail, or by special delivery or overnight mail.

This will cost more than if you send it by regular mail. If your letter weighs more than one ounce, you will need to pay extra postage, too. Letters to other countries cost more to send than mail to be delivered within the United States, Mexico, and Canada. Letters sent overseas may be sent by surface mail, which means they will go by boat. Airmail is more expensive but delivery is faster. If you don't know how much postage to use, a postal clerk will tell you.

Postcards

Sending postcards is an easy way to keep in touch with your friends when you are away on a vacation or trip.

Picture postcards usually have a scene of the place you are visiting. The other side of the card is divided into two parts. You write the name and address of your friend on

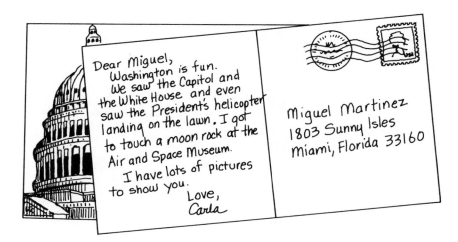

Dear Miguel,
Washington is fun.
We saw the Capitol and
the White House and even
saw the President's helicopter
landing on the lawn. I got
to touch a moon rock at the
Air and Space Museum.
   I have lots of pictures
to show you.
        Love,
        Carla

Miguel Martinez
1803 Sunny Isles
Miami, Florida 33160

the right-hand side of the card, and a short message on the left-hand side. The stamp is pasted above the address in the upper corner of the card.

Since there is so little space, a few words are enough to tell your friends and family you are thinking about them. You do not have to write your address, a salutation, or a close, or even the date. Just be sure to sign the card!

Postal Cards

Postal cards have no pictures. They are plain cards, sold by the post office, with a stamp already printed on the upper right-hand corner. Write the name and address of the person you are writing to and your return address on the stamp side of the card. The blank side of the postal card is for your message.

Do not write anything that is private on a postcard or postal card. When you have something to say that is private, write it in a letter that is sealed in an envelope.

ALL KINDS OF FRIENDLY LETTERS

Here are a few hints to help you get started writing friendly letters. Once you have had some practice, you will be able to do it easily.

Write about an interesting experience you have had. Your entire letter could be about this. Perhaps you have a new pet. You could tell how you got it and how you have been training it.

Families sometimes move from one place to another, to a different city or a different state or country. You could write about the change. Have you started at a new school? Describe what it is like. Have you made friends? Your letter could tell about the activities you plan or the things you hope to do.

1240 Marmonte Place
Venice, California 90230
September 29, 1988

Hi there, Michael,

I sure was glad to get your letter. Thanks for telling me all about the guys. Don't forget to tell everybody hello for me and tell them to write me too. I am friends with some guys a block away—they seem pretty cool—but I still miss the gang.

I like living here better now that we have a house. The motel my dad's company put us into— ugh!—what a joint! But the house is neat. We have a big backyard that is all fenced in, and guess what? We have a real orange tree and two lemon trees right in our own garden. The oranges taste pretty sour, though.

My dad put a basket up on the garage door and I have started practicing. I can sink balls a lot better now. Not like you of course. Anyway, not yet.

Los Angeles is a BIG place and the transportation stinks. They don't have any subways and we have to make so many changes on the bus, you wouldn't believe. Dad says my sister and I will get bicycles when Mom calms down a little.

I saved the best news for the last. I AM GETTING A DOG! I am going to train it myself too. What do you think I should call it?

Please write soon. Are you taking good care of my fish?

Your friend,
Leonard

Letters are the best way to keep in touch with relatives who do not live near you. Grandparents, especially, will treasure the letters you write.

458 Alpine Drive
Lost Hills, California 93249
March 16, 1988

Dear Grammy and Grandpop,
Estoy aprendiendo a leer y escribir en español. No puedo hablar bien.

That means, "I am learning to read and write in Spanish. I cannot speak well." At least I hope that is what I wrote. I am learning Spanish this year in school. My teacher comes from Costa Rica, which is a very small country close to South America.

There are many Hispanic families in Lost Hills. My best friend is Jesus. He comes from Mexico. He pronounces his name hay-soos. I never heard anyone in America called Jesus but he says in his country many boys are called by that name. He is a good swimmer and knows how to snorkel too. He is going to show me how and I am going to help him practice English.

I hope you are both well. Are you coming to visit this year?

Your loving grandson,
Allen

Writing a letter in the form of a diary is a good way to practice writing newsy letters. Tell about what you have done on each day of the week.

Dear Family,

Today is Monday the 12th. Grandpa met us at the train and we drove to the farm in his truck. They wanted Timmy to sleep with me on the porch. It has screens all around now and is just like a room, but Tim was scared. There is an owl in a tree that hoots. Also other noises. Grammy made him a bed on the living room couch. I guess he is still just a kid.

Tuesday. Gramps took us up to the timberline today. That is high in the mountains where the trees don't grow. We could see the whole valley below. We hiked and cooked hot dogs and Gramps showed Tim and me how to put out the cooking fire. After the fire is out you have to dig a shallow trench in a big circle all around it to make sure no cinders are left.

Wednesday. Grammy made us shell peas and pick vegetables. She made dumplings for supper. Grammy really knows how to cook.

Thursday. If we get our chores done, we get to go to the county fair tomorrow.

Saturday. Yesterday we went to the fair. There were rides and games and lots of different animals up for prizes. Uncle Fred won a prize for two of his chickens, and afterward he came back here for supper. He's a real neat guy. Tim fell climbing a tree. Got to go. Bye, now.

Love,
Stefan

P.S. Tim says hello.

Harry S. Truman was vice-president of the United States during Franklin Delano Roosevelt's fourth term as president. When President Roosevelt died suddenly on April 12, 1945, Truman became president. Even though he was very busy, Truman wrote regularly to his family in Missouri. He wrote this diary form of letter to his mother and aunt during the week he became president.

Blair House
April 1945

Dear Mama & Mary,

Well, I have had the most momentous and the most trying time anyone could possibly have, since Thursday, April 12th.

Maybe you'd like to know just what happened. We'd had a long, drawn out debate in the Senate and finally came to an agreement for a recess at 5 P.M. until Friday, Apr. 13th.

When I went back to my office, a call from Sam Rayburn, Speaker of the House, was awaiting me. Sam wanted me to come over to the House side of the Capitol and talk to him about policy and procedure and, as Alice in Wonderland would say, "shoes and ships and sealing wax and things". . . .

But—as soon as I came into the room Sam told me that Steve Early, the President's confidential press secretary wanted to talk to me. I called the White House, and Steve told me to come to the White House "as quickly and as quietly" as I could. . . .

When I arrived at the Pennsylvania entrance . . . a couple of ushers . . . took me up to Mrs. Roosevelt's study on the second floor.

. . . Mrs. Roosevelt put her arm on my shoulder and said, "Harry, the President is dead."

It was the only time in my life, I think, that I ever felt as if I'd had a real shock. I had hurried to the White House to see the President, and when I arrived, I found I was the President. No one in the history of our country ever had it happen to him just that way. . . .

Saturday afternoon, the White House funeral; Sunday morning the burial at Hyde Park, today my speech to Congress.

. . . My greatest trial was today when I addressed the Congress. It seemed to go over all right, from the ovation I received. Things have gone so well that I'm almost as scared as I was Thursday when Mrs. R. told me what had happened. Maybe it will come out all right.

Soon as we get settled in the White House you'll both be here to visit us. Lots of love from your very much worried son and bro.

Harry

If you find it hard to get started writing letters, you could practice by leaving short notes to members of your family. Here is a note a ten-year-old girl left one night for her parents to find:

Dear Tooth Fairy,

I worked very hard for this tooth. At first I thought that it wasn't supposed to come out. Then it hurt when I chewed so this tooth is worth a lot, plus I don't have many baby teeth left. So please, please, Please, PLEASE, give me equal payment for my pain!

And if you don't happen to have any tooth fairy money left from all the other people, just leave the money under my pillow some other night.

Sincerely,
Lara Clements

When you are away from home, the letters you get from your family and friends are especially welcome. You don't feel left out of things that are happening, even though you are away.

Keeping in touch works both ways. When you are away from home, your family and friends want to hear about *your* experiences. They also want to be sure you are all right. When your family and friends are away from home, *they* want to get mail from home, too.

Highland Boy Scouts #36
Calistoga, California 94515
August 6, 1988

Dear Isaac,

I am doing just fine up here and I have made lots of friends. The climate is hot! I have the lower bunk, but every week we change off.

I have done a lot of horseback riding. Eddie, our riding counselor, taught us how to lead a horse and how to stay in the saddle when galloping, and I can tie a horse up and mount and dismount all by myself.

If you want to know what animals I take care of, it's the mother duck and the baby ducks and the baby goats. Today for the first time we let the goats run around the ranch. My goat, Buffy, ate some paint thinner and we had to feed him salt milk out of a baby bottle. That's no easy job. He might die, or he will probably live.

The horses I have ridden so far are Captain (my favorite), Satin, and Patsy. I hate Angel Face because she is slow and uncooperative besides.

That's all so far.

With love from your cousin,
Teddy

P.S. The goat got well again and is very healthy. Please bring balloons when you come with my parents on visiting day. Great for water fights!

3054 Maple Street
Fernwood, Idaho 83830
July 23, 1988

Hi, Diane,

I got your letter yesterday and it sounds as if you are having fun. I wish I could go to the mountains. I get car sick. Dad says I will outgrow it. I bet!

Sandra and I take swimming lessons three mornings a week. We practice for thirty-five minutes and then have free time for twenty minutes. So far, I can float on my back, do a dead man's float, and see under water. They are teaching us the crawl.

Most afternoons I go to Rachel's house until my

mother or father gets home from work. Last night Mommy bought hot dogs and took me and Rachel to the park for a barbecue. Daddy promised to take us to the beach on Sunday.

I miss you. Do you miss me?

Your best friend,
Terry

MAKING FRIENDS THROUGH LETTERS

You could write to someone you have never met but would like to know. Many friendships have started in this way. One famous love story began when the poet Robert Browning wrote to the poet Elizabeth Barrett. His first letter started, "I love your verses with all my heart, dear Miss Barrett . . . and I love you too."

Here is a letter from a girl who wanted to be pen pals with a member of her family whom she had never met.

123 Juniper Avenue
Santa Cruz, California 95060
July 12, 1988

Dear Matthew,

You don't know me—yet. I hope you will someday. I am your mother's brother's daughter's child. I will now wait a minute to see if you can figure it out!

Did you? If you did, you know I am the granddaughter of Ted Timpone. My mom tells stories about her father and I wish I had known him. I thought it would be fun if his grandchildren could get to know the grandchildren of his sister. Do you like the idea?

I am ten years old and I'll be in the sixth grade in September. I am one grade ahead because I skipped kindergarten. I like to play the violin and I love to write letters. Mostly I love to receive them. I love school—especially math. I have a brother who is six years old and just can't wait until he is seven.

Please write back and tell me about yourself and what things you like to do. I would also like a picture of you.

Your cousin,
Rachel Hannah

After a terrible earthquake in Mexico City, students from many schools in the United States wrote to students in Mexico City to show sympathy. Some of the students have since become "letter friends." You, too, can make new friends by writing to pen pals in another school or another town or another country.

If you are studying a foreign language, your teacher might help you find a pen pal in a country where that language is spoken. You and your pen pal could practice each other's language, and a good friendship may develop.

107 Canon View Drive
Ojai, California 93023
October 14, 1988

Dear Pierre,

I am very happy you and I were matched up to be pen pals. You and your family sound very interesting.

In what part of France do you live? I could not find Fayence on my map.

The town where I live is very beautiful. It is in a valley and it is close to the Pacific Ocean. It is usually warm all year. The nearest large city is Los Angeles. We can drive there in an hour.

There are three children in my family, aged fourteen, twelve, and nine, all girls. I am in the middle. My father works in a citrus orchard. He hires people to pick oranges and lemons. My mother works in the town library three mornings a week.

My teacher thinks I should write to you in French and you should write to me in English from now on. Do you agree?

Je vieux dire une autre fois que je suis heureuse que vous êtes mon "ami de plume." J'éspère que nous serons amis vraiment.

Qu'est-ce que vous aimez faire le plus?

Your pen pal,
Eloise

P.S. Please tell me when I make mistakes in French.

———— THANK-YOU NOTES ————

Since you were very young, you have been receiving presents on one occasion or another. Only very small children take gifts for granted. As we grow older, we begin to understand that it takes time and thoughtfulness to choose the right presents.

Giving is one part of showing how we feel about people; how we receive is just as important. There is no set rule for how to say thank you, only that you should say it promptly. Be yourself and write what you feel. It is a good idea to mention something about the gift in the thank-you note.

Thank You for the Birthday Gift

Waipio Valley
Honokaa, Hawaii 96727
June 4, 1988

Dear Aunt Phyllis,

Thank you for the book of haiku poetry. I never heard the word haiku before, but my teacher said that good haiku poetry is hard to write because it has to be very short. Also you shouldn't use words that are not necessary.

I wrote a haiku for you.

My aunt's sweet gift of poems
Wakens my ear.
And I hear the music.

Thank you again, Aunt Phyllis. I hope you like my poem.

Your loving niece,
Jaia Rose

Thank You for the Christmas Gift

1810 Kleeman Avenue
So. Minneapolis, Minnesota 55405
December 27, 1988

Dear Lucy,

Thanks for the Christmas money. I got lots of presents this year and we all had a lot of fun. I wish you could have been with us.

My dad said I may spend your check any way I like, and that is the most exciting part of it.

Did you spend Christmas in Mexico? I hope you had a wonderful holiday.

Lots of love and kisses,
Rafe

At times you may receive a gift you cannot use or do not like, or it is something you already have. When that happens you feel disappointed. Even though the gift did not make you happy, someone was trying to please you.

Jane did not like the Christmas gift from her aunt, and she forgot to remember the thought behind the gift. This is what she wrote.

Dear Aunt Mary,

I just received the knitting bag you sent for Christmas. I do not like to knit, but thank you.

Love,
Jane

Jane *did* write an honest letter. And she said thank you. Can you think of a letter Jane could have written that was honest and also more kind?

Dear Aunt Mary,

    Thank you for the knitting bag. It was so nice of you to remember me at Christmas.

                         Love,
                         Jane

When You Want to Say Thank You Again

Do you sometimes get presents that cannot be used immediately? They may be gifts of money, or something you must grow into or that you have to learn how to use. Even though you sent a thank-you note when you first received the gift, you might want to write again. These letters show an extra special thoughtfulness.

               1810 Kleeman Avenue
               So. Minneapolis, Minnesota 55405
               March 2, 1988

Dear Lucy,

    When I thanked you for the check at Christmas I didn't know what I was going to get with it. I must have bought a million different things before I decided. I mean in my head. But yesterday my dad took me to the skateboard store. They were having a sale, but I decided to get the parts and put it together myself, with my dad's help, of course.

I bought a deck and trucks and wheels. My dad got me grip tape and rails. You should see it, Lucy! I wish you could.

I gave my mom my old board and she is going to learn to skateboard. I already gave her one lesson. I think maybe she'll make it.

Hope you come to visit soon.

Rafe

When You Have Been a Guest

Kathy visited her grandparents one Easter vacation. She flew 3,000 miles to be with them, and all her grandparents' friends and family planned activities to make it a happy vacation.

After Kathy returned home her mother reminded her to write her "bread-and-butter letters." Bread and butter is an expression for a letter that says thank you to the people you have visited. Even though you thanked everyone in person, it is good to thank them again in writing.

April 15, 1988

Dear Grandma and Grandpa,

You gave me the very best vacation I can ever remember. It was interesting to visit all the places I used to know when I was little and to see where I was born, though I didn't honestly remember them from when I was little.

I had such a good time, I wish I could do it all over again. I love you, and I think you are the best grandparents that ever were.

Kisses,
Kathy

1506 Magnolia Street
Chehalis, Washington 98532
August 23, 1988

Dear Alicia,

It was nice of you to let me spend the day with you and Dora. I would never have gotten to see Chicago since Mom and Dad both had all day meetings. Best of all, it was wonderful to have someone my own age to be with. Thanks for taking me to the museum, too. Chicago looks like a pretty nice place. I liked the lake shore the best, and next to that I loved riding on the elevated train.

I hope you will visit Washington soon and that you will bring Dora with you. We could show you many pretty places. Please tell Dora I send love and kisses.

Thanks, again.

Sincerely,
Pamela

WHEN SOMEONE IS SICK

There are times when you need to stay home because of an accident or illness. You may have a contagious disease that keeps friends from visiting you. Don't spend your time feeling sorry for yourself. The U.S. mails will take you out of quarantine. So *write, don't gripe!* Thank your friends for their notes and telephone calls. Let them know that you are glad they think of you. Your letters will keep you part of the gang.

April 18, 1988

Dear Bill,

This letter is for all the fellows who sent me letters and cards while I've been home with the chicken pox. It's great that everybody remembered me. It's pretty boring being home, but I think the doctor is letting me out on Tuesday.

Sorry I missed the play. Who took my part?

Would you believe? I can't wait to get back to school!

Your polka-dotted friend,
Mark

12805 Crest Drive
Tangent, Oregon 97389
November 13, 1988

Dear Ms. Ostrow,

Thank you for the book. I saw the movie but I had never read "Heidi" before, and I enjoyed it very much.

I was happy that your letter said you and the class miss me.

Love,
Gretchen Hoffman

If, by chance, your friends have neglected you, there is nothing wrong with reminding them.

Thursday

Hey, you guys,

It's no fun being tied up in traction with no one to talk to and nothing but dumb shows on TV.

What about coming to see me? Or at least write me and tell me what's going on in good old P.S. 64. There is still room for a hundred autographs on my cast.

Your lonely pal,
Stevie

When your friends are ill they need to be remembered by you. A short note will help to cheer them up. Write about how you miss them and tell them about all the things that are going on.

April 5, 1988

Dear Jeremy,

All the kids miss you at school. I wanted to come to see you but I never got shots for mumps. I am going to get them for sure now.

We started practice yesterday and Mr. Anderson is saving first base for you. Bill Thomas has it until you come back. He sure has butterfingers, but he tries, I guess. We play the fifth grade next week, so you better get well soon. We need you.

Your friend,
Larry

May 12, 1988

Dear Mrs. Pinkham,

I hope you are feeling better and will be out of the hospital soon. My brother can't write yet, but he hopes so too. We had a good time when we visited you last month.

Sincerely,
Tony

——— WHEN SOMEONE DIES ———

When there has been a death in a family, the letter one writes to express sympathy is called a condolence letter. A condolence letter is an expression of friendship and is a way of holding out your hand to a friend who is sad.

Even adults have a hard time writing a condolence letter. But if you say only that you are sorry, your friend will feel comforted by your thought.

If you want to say more, try to imagine that you have just met your friend on the street. What would you say? You could write that.

November 23, 1988

Dear Tony,

My mother told me your father died. I hope you will not be too sad. I am very sorry about it. I liked your father very much.

Love,
Marlene

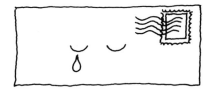

April 3, 1988

Dear Grammy,

I am sorry that Grandpop died. He was really kind and he did things well. I remember him in my mind even though I never got to see him much.

Whenever I feel real bad about him I think to myself that even though I am sad that he died, there will still be good things in my life. I hope you will not be lonely.

Love,
Jesse Josef

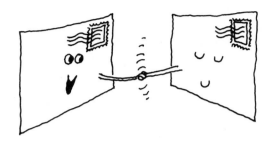

— CONGRATULATIONS! —

When you hear good news about a friend or a member of your family, it makes you happy too. We all like to share the happiness or good luck of a friend. Writing a letter of congratulation shows friends that you share their pleasure. Here are a few hints about how to do it.

1. Tell why you are congratulating your friend. Don't say, "I just heard the good news," but mention what the good news is.
2. Express your pleasure in the good news.
3. Be natural. Be yourself.

May 15, 1988

Dear Aunt Mary:

    I just heard about your engagement and I am thrilled! I know you are going to be very happy. Is he good-looking? Please send a picture.

    When is the wedding? Are young people going to be invited? (Hint, hint.)

With love and kisses,
Leah

32 Linden Lane
Rocky Point, Arizona 71901
June 4, 1988

Dear George,

The whole family watched you on television this afternoon and I bet you could hear the shouting clear to California. Wow, but you sure were in great form! The last dive was a zinger! I just knew you were going to win and you deserve it.

The whole family send congratulations. We are so proud of you!

Your proud and loving cousin,
Gertrude

——— HOW TO SAY ——— YOU'RE SORRY

No one is perfect. We all make mistakes. It's no great shame if you make a mistake, but it is a pity if you can't admit it. Often you can wipe away the sting of a mistake by admitting your error. For some people this is hard to do face to face. A short note may be easier.

January 23, 1988

Dear Johnny,

I'm really sorry I bent the wheels of your skateboard. I have made that jump a million times and I don't know how I could have missed.

Dad is going to help me earn the money to get you new wheels.

I hope you're not sore.

Your friend,
Norman

July 3, 1988

Dear May,

I am too embarrassed to look you in the face. I was so sure I had returned your umbrella long ago. Yesterday my sister found it in our snow closet. It was there all the time. I had looked in the snow closet too, but the umbrella was way in the back behind my brother's skis.

Do you need it now or can it wait until vacation is over? I can mail it to you if you need it now. Let me know.

Please forgive me.

Your friend-with-the-red-face,
Emily

ANGRY LETTERS

There is a very easy rule about writing angry letters to a friend. It has one word: Don't! If you must write an angry letter to a friend, don't mail it.

If you have written a letter in anger, put it aside for a day or two. Then read it over and remember that the best reason for writing an angry letter to a friend is to make a bad situation better so that you can go on being friends. When you have read the letter over carefully, ask yourself: have you left room for your friend to explain his or her side? Have you said things that can never be taken back? Does your letter sound even angrier than you meant it to?

Perhaps this story will help you decide whether to send your angry letter. Benjamin Franklin, a great hero of the American Revolution, was also a great letter writer. He wrote often to a friend in England. When the war broke out between England and the new American colonies, Franklin was so angry at England and all the English that he wrote and accused his friend of having American blood on his hands. Franklin did not, however, mail the letter. When the American Revolutionary War was over, Franklin and his English friend began writing to each other again.

So if you must write an angry letter, do. Get it out of your system. But don't mail it.

Angry Letters by a Public Citizen

There is a different rule about angry letters written to people who are in the public eye, like government officials or newspaper and television personalities. Speaking up—for yourself, for your community, or for your ideas—is an act of a responsible person. In Ancient Greece such a person was called a "public citizen"—a title of great honor and respect.

When you write an angry letter to a government official, to a public figure, or a corporation, your reader will pay more attention to you if your letter is fair. There is nothing wrong with showing that you are angry, but you must state clearly why you are angry. Demand an explanation or ask to have the problem looked at.

When you write to strangers, follow the style for business letters. (See page 22.)

1215 Lincoln Place
Building 3E
Brooklyn, New York 11236
October 23, 1988

The Honorable John Doakes
United States House of Representatives
Washington, D. C. 20515

Dear Representative Doakes:

My class is studying the rules on voting used by the Congress. We are puzzled by the way Congress allowed itself to be given a raise in salary without voting for it. We think this is a real cop-out, and that anyone who was really against a salary increase would have found a way to stop it, or at least make an issue of it.

My class and I are puzzled about other matters too.

With respect, Sir, we do not understand how you could accept a raise in salary and vote against school lunches. We do not understand how you can accept a raise in your salary and never say one word about the homeless. We do not understand how you can accept a raise in salary and cut down on help to old people.

If you have an explanation, my class and I would like to hear it.

Respectfully,
Daniel Shaftell

1260 Mission Street
Santa Rosa, California 95404
April 26, 1988

General Manager
United States Post Office
Rincon Annex
San Francisco, California 94104

Dear Post Office General Manager:

I want to complain about how junk mail is delivered. Lots of advertisements and catalogs are delivered almost every day. The mail carriers put them all together. That is, they stuff the small stuff inside fat pieces of mail. The trouble is they also stuff magazines inside the junk mail too.

My parents complain about junk mail all the time. My mom just throws it all away. Last week she accidentally threw away my stamp-collecting magazine.

The mail carrier told me that junk mail gives lots of people jobs. I don't want to hurt anyone, but I think the postal workers should separate junk mail from magazines.

I think you should have a new sorting system. The post office tells us to use zip code numbers because it helps the post office. Well, I think you should do something for us, too!

Sincerely,
Nerlindo Gutteriez

WRITING TO FAMOUS PEOPLE

The men and women who run our government are familiar to us because we hear and read about their work. So are some actors, singers, athletes, dancers, and writers. They have become public figures. Some people become public figures because they have devoted their lives to helping other people.

When you have done something well, you want to be noticed and praised for it. When public figures have pleased you, they like to know about it, too.

Don't be self-conscious about writing to someone just because that person is famous. Public figures do not usually get to meet the people they are working for, or trying to entertain, or teach, and it is from your letters that they learn that they have pleased or displeased you.

Even so busy a person as the President of the United States wants to know what people are thinking. In 1860, a very young girl, Grace Bedell, wrote to Abraham Lincoln and told him she thought he would look better with a beard. President Lincoln wrote back promptly:

October 19, 1860

My dear little Miss,

    Your very agreeable letter of the 15th is received. I regret the necessity of saying I have no daughters. I have three sons—one seventeen, one nine, and one seven years of age. They, with their mother, constitute my whole family.

    As to the whiskers, having never worn any, do you not think people would call it a piece of silly affectation if I were to begin now?

Your sincere well wisher,
A. Lincoln

After President Lincoln wrote this letter, he must have thought some more about Grace Bedell's suggestion, for he grew a beard after all!

2807 Western Place
Elmwood, Louisiana 70112
October 19, 1988

Mr. Bruce Springsteen
CBS Records
New York, NY 10019

Dear Bruce Springsteen:

    My friend gave me a cassette of you singing *Born in the U.S.A.* and I liked it so much I took it to school for my classmates to enjoy too. Everyone already knew it but we played it during our music class anyway.

I have heard this song on the radio many times, and I love the way you sing it.

Sincerely yours,

Theodore Weppler

Theodore Weppler

P. S. I also like the book about you, *Born to Run.*

24 Ocean Avenue
Lakeville, Illinois 60045
February 14, 1988

The President
The White House
Washington, D. C. 20500

Dear Mr. President:

In our school we had a discussion about your speech calling for a better education program. We agree with you, Mr. President. Our school has to have half-day sessions for the lower three grades because there is not enough room. We also agree that if there were more teachers it would be better.

We were wondering, Mr. President, how we will be able to get more teachers and room for the lower grades to go to school full time if there is never enough money to pay for them? Everyone says they are in favor of education, but why don't they support the schools with money?

We cannot vote yet but if we could, we would vote to support your program for more schools and more teachers. We think every child should have a good education.

Respectfully yours,
Rebecca Coffee

——— INVITATIONS AND HOW ———
TO ANSWER THEM

Invitations are fun to receive and fun to send because almost always invitations are sent to friends to share a happy event.

The kind of invitation you send depends on whether or not you like to make your own invitations, what materials you have, and the kind of party you are giving. You can buy invitations in a store, write them on a card or a sheet of stationery, or design them yourself.

An invitation should include the following information: What the invitation is for, the time, the place, the date, and your name. Invitations should be sent out two weeks before the party, if possible. In that way you and your guests will have time to make plans.

Try to mail all your invitations at the same time so none of your friends will be hurt, wondering about being left out.

If you buy invitations, you may want to write a note to show your friends you really want them to come.

When Grover Cleveland was president of the United States, he sent this handwritten invitation to a few close friends.

Washington, D.C.
May 29, 1886

Dear ——

I am to be married on Wednesday evening at seven o'clock at the White House to Miss Folsom. It will be a very quiet affair and I will be extremely gratified at your attendance on this occasion.

Sincerely yours,
Grover Cleveland

Notice how simply yet warmly the President made all his guests feel wanted and welcome.

Good manners require that you reply to invitations promptly. Some invitations have the letters R.S.V.P. in the lower left-hand corner. This is an abbreviation for a French phrase, *Répondez, s'il vous plaît.* These words, which mean "Reply, if you please," tell you that your friend needs to know whether or not you are coming to the party. You should reply as soon as you can.

There is a good reason why you should reply promptly. It takes time to plan a good party. One has to know how many guests to expect and how much ice cream to order. It's hard to plan games without knowing how many players will show up.

If a telephone number appears underneath the R.S.V.P., you are expected to reply by telephone. If an address appears under the R.S.V.P., your friend wants you to reply by mail.

Did you notice that President Cleveland did not write R.S.V.P. on his invitation? Can you imagine anyone refusing an invitation from the president of the United States?

February 2, 1988

Dear Richie,

    This year I am going to celebrate my birthday by spending a weekend in the snow. At least I hope there's going to be snow! My mother and father are taking me and three boys, and I would like you to be one of them. We are going to rent a cabin at Bull Run State Park and go cross-country skiing. My father will rent skis for us. Maybe some sleds too. I hope you can come.

    We are leaving from my house on Saturday, February 20, at 9:00 A.M. and expect to return about 7:00 P.M. on Sunday.

    Please let me know if you can come.

Your friend,
David

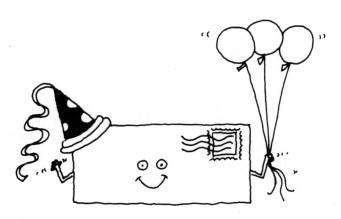

2345 Post Street
San Antonio, Texas
June 12, 1988

Hi Mark,

I have an offer you can't refuse. Our school is raising money by having a big car-washing marathon on the last Saturday of this month. The Handy Carwash on Elm Street—you remember? right opposite the Y—is letting us use their equipment and their parking lot, and their head honcho is going to supervise. Four students will work on each car, and the team that washes the most cars will win a prize. If you come, Pogo and Mike and you and I will be one team. After the marathon we are going to Pete's Pizza.

Can you come? You could take a bus Friday after school and my dad will drive you home after dinner on Sunday.

Hope to see you,
Emelio

Answering an Invitation

February 5, 1988

Dear David,

You can bet I'll be at your place on Saturday the 20th, with all my gear.

Thanks a lot for asking me. I hope there will be lots of snow so we can have a snowball fight.

See you Saturday,
Richie

June 18, 1988

Dear Emelio,

Rotten luck! I can't come. I really wanted to see you and the guys. But my dad got laid off and we may have to move to another city. He is taking the whole family that weekend to show Mom a place he found.

It is not far from where my aunt Lucy lives and where my dad will probably get a new job, so maybe it'll be okay with Mom. It sure won't with me. Maybe he won't get the job. I'll let you know what happens.

Your friend,
Mark

SOME BUSINESS LETTERS

1167 Webster Avenue
Scarsdale, New York 10583
February 13, 1988

The New York Times
229 West 43 Street
New York, New York 10036

Dear Publisher:

Our class is putting out the school paper this year. We would like to visit your plant to see how your newspaper is published. There are twenty-six in our class, including our teacher. One or two parents may also come along.

If it is possible for us to visit, please let us know when we may come and approximately how much time you will be able to give us.

Yours truly,
Miss Salit's Class
By: *Jeffrey Jablonski*

4456 Marmonte Lane
San Miguel, New Mexico 88058
April 8, 1988

Franklin Watts, Inc.
387 Park Avenue South
New York, New York 10016

Dear Publisher:

    I found a book in the library called *Let's Go to Greece* and I wonder if you have books about other countries that are written for young people.

    If you have a catalog, please send me one.

Yours truly,
John Contini

56 Cedar Lane
Jackson, Mississippi 39203
March 5, 1988

Mr. Revels Cayton
202 Eastern Avenue
Seattle Heights, Washington 98063

Dear Mr. Cayton:

    I am writing a paper for my class in Black History and I would like your help. I found out that you are the grandson of Hiram Revels, the first black senator in the U. S. Senate. He was also president of a college in Mississippi.

I would like to know if you would record on a cassette tape any stories that you know about your grandfather. Also I would like to know about you and your family. Were you born in Mississippi? Did you know your grandfather while he was alive? Do you know any stories about your grandmother? Where were you raised? What did your parents do? Were both your parents black? Did your parents tell you stories about your grandfather when you were growing up?

I hope you don't think I am too pushy, but I want to write a good paper. We are very proud of Hiram Revels in this state, but I don't know too much about him. I will appreciate any help you can give me.

Cordially,
Samantha Washington

P. S. I am enclosing a blank cassette and a stamped and addressed envelope.

A POSTSCRIPT

All through this book, we have talked about how your letters will please your friends and family and how a letter from you may be a gift of your friendship.

But writing letters can be a gift to yourself too. As you practice expressing yourself on paper, you will begin to enjoy the pleasure of using words well. And the more often you write letters, the better you will be able to communicate to your friends—and to yourself—your thoughts and feelings.

How to
Punctuate Letters

When you write letters, follow the same rules of punctuation that are used in other kinds of writing.

Capital Letters

Begin each sentence with a capital letter. Capitalize the first letter of a name of a person, place, or thing. Use a capital letter for the word "I." Begin the first word and each important word in the title of a book, poem, or story with a capital letter.

The titles of books, plays, and long poems should be underlined. For newspapers, magazines, and books, titles are set in italic type. As we can't do that in writing or typing, we underline the titles.

In the salutation of a letter, each word begins with a capital.

Dear Mr. Smith:
Dear Ms. Hunt:

However, in the close of a letter only the first word of the close begins with a capital.

Cordially yours,
Yours truly,

The Period (.)

As in other writing, all sentences end with a punctuation mark. A statement is followed by a period.
Place a period after these titles:

Dr. Mr. Mrs. Ms.

Each initial in a name is followed by a period.

Angela S. Weppler
R. H. McLennan

An abbreviation is followed by a period.

Sun. Aug. lb. N.Y.

The Comma (,)

Place a comma between:

The names of a city and state   Upland, Iowa
The day and the year in a date   July 4, 1776

Place a comma after:

The salutation in a friendly letter   Dear Karyn,
The close of a letter   With love,

The Question Mark (?)

A question mark follows a sentence that asks a question, such as: Can you come to my party?

The Exclamation Point (!)

An exclamation point is used after sentences or words that exclaim, that is, they express excitement or surprise: Oh, he came after all!

Quotation Marks (" ")

To quote means to repeat the words spoken or written by someone. The words quoted are called the quotation. Quotation marks are placed before and after the quotation to set it off from the rest of the sentence: Abigail said, "I am going to the library after school."

A comma is used to separate the quotation from the words telling who said it. The first word of a quoted sentence begins with a capital letter.

The Colon (:)

The colon is used after the salutation in a business letter.

Dear Dr. Stone:
Dear Editor:

Paragraphs

Unless you are using a typewriter or personal computer, indent the first line of a paragraph. If you are typing, you may start every line at the left margin, but only if you always leave a full line space between paragraphs. Start a new paragraph when you begin a new thought.

How to Abbreviate
State Names

The names of states and territories should not be abbreviated within the text of a letter. You may abbreviate the name of a state on the heading or inside address, but it is better not to on the envelope.

If you examine the list that follows, you can see that many state abbreviations look alike. If you do abbreviate, the abbreviations in the first column, from Webster's dictionary, are safer to use.

The two-letter abbreviations in the second column (to be used with the zip code) are preferred by the United States Post Office. This is because the automated sorting machines used by the Post Office can recognize only a two-letter abbreviation. Both letters are capitalized and are written without periods.

Alabama	Ala.	AL
Alaska	Alas.	AK
American Samoa	Amer. Samoa	AS
Arizona	Ariz.	AZ
Arkansas	Ark.	AR
California	Calif.	CA
Colorado	Colo.	CO
Connecticut	Conn.	CT
Delaware	Del.	DE
District of Columbia	D.C.	DC
Florida	Fla.	FL
Georgia	Ga.	GA
Guam	Guam	GU
Hawaii	Hawaii	HI
Idaho	Ida.	ID

Illinois	Ill.	IL
Indiana	Ind.	IN
Iowa	Ia.	IA
Kansas	Kans.	KS
Kentucky	Ky.	KY
Louisiana	La.	LA
Maine	Me.	ME
Maryland	Md.	MD
Massachusetts	Mass.	MA
Michigan	Mich.	MI
Minnesota	Minn.	MN
Mississippi	Miss.	MS
Missouri	Mo.	MO
Montana	Mont.	MT
Nebraska	Nebr.	NE
Nevada	Nev.	NV
New Hampshire	N.H.	NH
New Jersey	N.J.	NJ
New Mexico	N.Mex.	NM
New York	N.Y.	NY
North Carolina	N.C.	NC
North Dakota	N.Dak.	ND
Ohio	O.	OH
Oklahoma	Okla.	OK
Oregon	Oreg.	OR
Pennsylvania	Pa.	PA
Puerto Rico	P.R.	PR
Rhode Island	R.I.	RI
South Carolina	S.C.	SC
South Dakota	S.Dak.	SD
Tennessee	Tenn.	TN
Texas	Tex.	TX

Utah	Ut.	UT
Vermont	Vt.	VT
Virginia	Va.	VA
Virgin Islands	V.I.	VI
Washington	Wash.	WA
West Virginia	W.Va.	WV
Wisconsin	Wis.	WI
Wyoming	Wyo.	WY

Some Forms of Address

The following forms show how to address letters to public officials. In the salutation you may use the official's title alone (Dear Mr. President), or the official's title and name (Dear President Doe).

The President

The President
The White House
Washington, DC 20500

Dear President Doe:

The Vice-President

The Vice-President
Old Executive Office Building
17th Street and Pennsylvania Avenue
Washington, DC 20501

Dear Vice-President Smith:

The Chief Justice

The Chief Justice
The Supreme Court
1–1st Street N.E.
Washington, DC 20543

Dear Chief Justice:

Associate Justice

Justice Roberta Hunter
The Supreme Court
1–1st Street N.E.
Washington, DC 20543

Dear Justice Hunter:

Senator

The Honorable Amelia Finkel
United States Senator
Senate Office Building
Washington, DC 20510

Dear Senator Finkel:

Congressional Representative

The Honorable Augustus Hawkins
House of Representatives
Rayburn Building
Washington, DC 20515

Dear Representative Hawkins:

Secretary of Labor

The Honorable Sam Smith
Secretary of Labor
Department of Labor
Washington, D.C. 20210

Dear Mr. Secretary:

Governor

The Honorable Judith Prince
Governor of California
State Capitol
Sacramento, California 95814

Dear Governor Prince:

Mayor

The Honorable Richard Block
Mayor of the City of New York
City Hall
New York, New York 10007

Dear Mayor Block:

INDEX

ABOUT THE AUTHOR

Florence D. Mischel worked in Hollywood as an editor, story doctor, and occasional writer for radio, television, and motion pictures. She has edited and produced documentaries for public radio based on conferences recorded at the Center for the Study of Democratic Institutions in Santa Barbara, California. During the mid-1960s, the Center concentrated on a study of the First Amendment to the Constitution. Ms. Mischel became so interested in these studies that she enrolled in law school—as the oldest student to be admitted up to that time. At sixty-two, she began to practice labor law and describes her work as the practical application of the First Amendment to labor-management relations.

Now semiretired, Ms. Mischel divides her time between volunteer work and writing.